What's New
with
Dinosaur Fossils?

by Laura Johnson

PEARSON

Scott
Foresman

Editorial Offices: Glenview, Illinois • Parsippany, New Jersey • New York, New York
Sales Offices: Needham, Massachusetts • Duluth, Georgia • Glenview, Illinois
Coppell, Texas • Ontario, California • Mesa, Arizona

Photographs

Every effort has been made to secure permission and provide appropriate credit for photographic material. The publisher deeply regrets any omission and pledges to correct errors called to its attention in subsequent editions.

Unless otherwise acknowledged, all photographs are the property of Pearson Education, Inc.

Photo locators denoted as follows: Top (T), Center (C), Bottom (B), Left (L), Right (R), Background (Bkgd)

Illustrations Janet Skiles

ISBN: 0-328-13540-2

The Age of Dinosaurs

Dinosaurs first appeared on Earth approximately 228 million years ago. For about 160 million years, hundreds of different dinosaur species flourished on our planet. Scientists have designated this period of time the Mesozoic Era, though some call it "The Age of Dinosaurs."

About 65 million years ago, dinosaurs mysteriously became extinct. As the time line shows, dinosaurs did not exist at the same time as people. In fact, until the early 1800s, people didn't even know that dinosaurs had existed!

Now, however, we know a lot about dinosaurs. We are aware that some dinosaurs walked on two legs and others walked on four; that some were meat eaters and others were plant eaters; that some stood taller than four-story buildings and others were as small as chickens. How do we know all this? Through the work of paleontologists!

Diplodocus was one of the longest dinosaurs. It was longer than six cars lined up end-to-end. *Compsognathus*, at the size of a chicken, was one of the smallest.

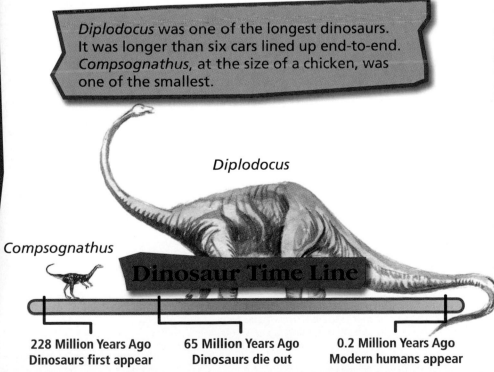

Diplodocus

Compsognathus

Dinosaur Time Line

228 Million Years Ago	65 Million Years Ago	0.2 Million Years Ago
Dinosaurs first appear	Dinosaurs die out	Modern humans appear

Paleontology and Dinosaurs

Paleontologists study forms of life that existed in prehistoric times, as revealed by the fossil record. The word *fossil* comes from the Latin *fossilis,* which means "dug up" or "obtained by digging," and indeed most fossils are found by digging or cutting through dirt, sand, clay, or rock. Fossils exist of insects, fish, clams, leaves, trees, and more, but the fossils that are best known by the public at large are dinosaur fossils.

Dinosaur paleontologists primarily examine body fossils and trace fossils left by dinosaurs in order to piece together clues about life millions of years ago. Body fossils include preserved bones, teeth, other body parts, and eggs, while trace fossils consist of such things as tracks, footprints, and bite marks–things that are not part of a dinosaur but that have left a trace of the dinosaur's activities.

Through their analysis of fossils, paleontologists have identified slightly more than 300 species of dinosaurs. This number continues to grow, as paleontologists have been discovering new dinosaur species at a rate of seven a year.

Before reading about dinosaur paleontologists' latest discoveries, let's start with a little background on early paleontologists.

Footprints, which are trace fossils, can provide a surprising amount of information about a dinosaur's size, weight, and speed.

These *Tyrannosaurus rex* teeth, some measuring as long as nine inches, are body fossils. A *Tyrannosaurus rex* could tear off five hundred pounds of food in a single bite!

Paleontology's Pioneers

People have been finding fossils for hundreds, possibly thousands, of years. However, the science of paleontology is only about 200 years old. It dates to the early 1800s, when the French scientist Georges Cuvier did the first systematic study of fossils. Dinosaurs, however, were first identified in England.

Dr. Gideon Mantell

Dr. Gideon Mantell was an **avid** fossil collector. In the early 1800s, he and his wife and scientific **collaborator** Mary Ann Mantell discovered several teeth embedded in rocks in southern England. While most scientists of the day thought the teeth must belong to a large, rare fish or mammal, Mantell believed they belonged to an as yet unknown creature. Because the teeth showed similarities to the teeth of modern iguanas, Mantell named the creature *Iguanadon*, meaning "iguana tooth."

About this same time, Mary Anning was collecting fossils along the south coast of England. She made several important discoveries and became known as the greatest fossil collector in the world. Interest in fossils was exploding.

In the mid-1800s, British doctor and paleontologist Sir Richard Owen was asked to catalog the fossil collection of the British royal family. As he worked, he realized that three fossils in the collection were not only different from any animals living at the time but also distinct from any fossils he had studied before.

An expert in anatomy, Owen noticed that the legs of the reptiles whose fossils he was studying were significantly different from the legs of modern reptiles. He came to the conclusion that the fossils belonged to a group of extinct reptiles.

Sir Richard Owen

Because these newly identified reptiles were so massive, Owen called them *dinosaurs,* which is Greek for "terrible lizard." People were soon using Owen's name for all of the extinct lizards they discovered–and are still discovering.

Dinosaurs' legs are angled differently from those of modern reptiles.

7

Paleontologists believe that *Giganotosaurus* was even bigger than *Tyrannosaurus rex*.

Tyrannosaurus rex's short arms have puzzled paleontologists for years. The arms were too short to reach the dinosaur's mouth, so they could not be used for feeding purposes.

Giganotosaurus: Bigger than *T. Rex*

For decades, paleontologists thought that *Tyrannosaurus rex* was the largest carnivorous, or meat-eating, dinosaur to have ever roamed the planet. However, in 1995 fossil hunters in Argentina found a skull and leg bones belonging to a carnivore that scientists have since determined was probably even larger than *Tyrannosaurus rex.*

Paleontologists named the dinosaur *Giganotosaurus,* meaning "giant southern lizard," because of its size and where it was found. Although bigger than *Tyrannosaurus rex,* scientists think *Giganotosaurus* had a smaller brain, less powerful jaws, and narrower teeth than its better-equipped relative, deficiencies that might have made it a less efficient predator than *T. Rex.* These two giants lived on different continents and were separated by millions of years, so they would never have met.

Tyrannosaurus rex, despite being a little smaller than the *Giganotosaurus,* was a fearsome killer that grew to more than forty feet in length and weighed seven tons or more. Its hind legs tapered off to powerful, birdlike claws, and its short arms had two sharp claws. Equipped with deadly teeth, *Tyrannosaurus rex*'s huge jaws were its most lethal weapon.

Scientists are studying trace fossils of *Tyrannosaurus rex* to determine how fast it moved. Some think it sprinted quickly for short distances to catch prey, while others believe it could only travel at a fast walk. Examining the distances between footprints may help solve this mystery.

Seismosaurus: The Earth Shaker

Just as paleontologists have been compelled to revise their views regarding the largest carnivorous dinosaur, so too have they altered their ideas concerning the largest **herbivorous,** or plant-eating, dinosaur. Previously, paleontologists had considered *Brachiosaurus,* which grew to about 90 feet long and weighed up to 80 tons, the largest plant eater. Then, in 1979, fossil hunters in New Mexico excavated fossils of an even larger dinosaur. Named *Seismosaurus,* or "earth-shaking lizard," this plant eater may have grown to be 120 feet long and weigh 90 tons.

One of the most intriguing (and controversial) theories regarding *Seismosaurus* is that it could swing its tail fast enough to generate a sonic boom, similar to those made by supersonic jets. Scientists who believe this think *Seismosaurus* used the sound to scare off predators and communicate with other dinosaurs.

Paleontologists have developed several more fascinating theories about plant eaters based on the fossil remains

of *Seismosaurus*. One of these theories involves a pile of stomach stones that were found in the parts of the fossils where the dinosaur's stomach would have been. Paleontologists take these gastroliths as a sign that *Seismosaurus* deliberately swallowed stones to help digest the plant leaves that it ate. The stones would have ground against the leaves sitting in the dinosaur's stomach, in the process breaking the leaves down into smaller, easier-to-digest pieces.

New discoveries are being made all the time. *Seismosaurus* was huge, but several other monsters are in **contention** for the title of "biggest dinosaur." For many of these giants, no complete skeletons have been found, so it's hard to know exactly how long or tall they were. Also, we don't know if the skeletons we have represent the largest specimens. But even if we don't know who was the most massive, we can be amazed at the size of these giants.

Seismosaurus, estimated to have been 120 feet long and to weigh 90 tons, was a huge dinosaur.

New Discoveries and New Ideas About Dinosaurs

Until recently, the scientific **consensus** was that, like all modern lizards, dinosaurs were cold blooded. This means that the temperature of their blood changes with the temperature of their surroundings. Cold-blooded animals are warmed by the sun (which makes them more energetic) and cooled by the shade (which makes them more lethargic), while warm-blooded animals maintain a constant temperature. This makes it possible for warm-blooded animals, such as birds and mammals, to adapt to different environments. Fur and feathers help warm-blooded animals maintain their body temperatures.

In 1996 scientists in China unearthed a fossil that challenged the idea that all dinosaurs were cold blooded. The small fossil, named *Sinosauropteryx,* showed feather-like markings. This led many paleontologists to conclude that, if these markings indeed were the remains of feathers, this dinosaur may have been warm blooded. If one species of warm-blooded dinosaur existed, there most likely were others.

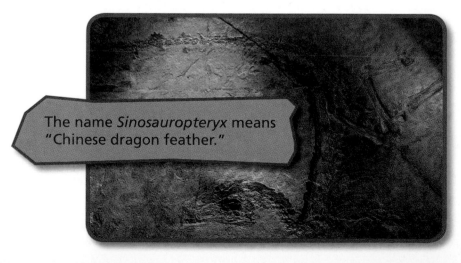

The name *Sinosauropteryx* means "Chinese dragon feather."

More *Sinosauropteryx* fossils have been found in the past decade. The fossilized food found in their stomachs indicates that these dinosaurs ate lizards and mammals. One *Sinosauopteryx* had two fossilized eggs inside her body, proving that, like many other dinosaurs, this species laid eggs.

For a long time, paleontologists did not know whether dinosaurs formed social groups or cared for their young. In the early 1900s, fossils of large groups of *Protoceratops* were found in Mongolia. These dinosaurs could have been living or traveling in a group when they died. In 1978 a paleontologist discovered fossils of baby dinosaurs and young dinosaurs near a fossilized nest, which seemed to indicate that some dinosaurs raised their young until they could survive on their own. The paleontologist was so impressed by this evidence of dinosaurs protecting and nurturing their young that he named the fossil (which belonged to a species of dinosaur previously unknown to science) *Maiasuara,* which means "good mother lizard."

A model of a piece of ground showing *Allosaurus* and *Apatosaurus* footprints

Recently discovered fossil footprints belonging to a dinosaur named *Apatosaurus* seem to indicate that *Maiasaura* was not the only dinosaur to care for its young. The footprints, called **trackways**, show a mixture of small and large dinosaur footprints. Although it's possible that the trackways were made by smaller (instead of younger) dinosaurs, scientists have interpreted them as proof that *Apatosaurus* parents traveled with their offspring.

There's also evidence that dinosaurs communicated, as structures found in fossilized dinosaur skulls may have been used to emit snarls, squeaks, grunts, and similar message-sending noises.

Name That Dinosaur!

Have you noticed that the names of dinosaurs often describe a particular trait or feature about the dinosaur, such as "iguana tooth," "good mother lizard," and "earth-shaker"? Usually, dinosaurs are named for their qualities or where they were found. The scientific name of a dinosaur also often includes the name of the discoverer. Christopher Wolfe had a dinosaur named after him when he was eight years old! Christopher was with his father, a paleontologist, when he noticed something blackish-purple sticking out of the dirt. That "something" turned out to be the fossilized horn of a previously unknown dinosaur, that was later named *Zuniceratops christopheri*!

Depending on the species that laid them, dinosaur eggs were either round or pointed, and ranged in size from less than one inch to more than eighteen inches in length.

Dinosaurs in Alaska?

In 1985 fossils of eight species of dinosaurs were found in Alaska. This surprised scientists, because dinosaurs normally required tropical or temperate conditions. However, a study of plant fossils soon showed that Alaska was much warmer millions of years ago. Still, though warmer than today, Alaska was cooler than other dinosaur habitats. Also, the amount of daylight changes dramatically between summer and winter. Closer study of the fossils led scientists to hypothesize that one species may have adapted to reduced winter light–but what about the others? Scientists still wonder how Alaska's dinosaurs survived.

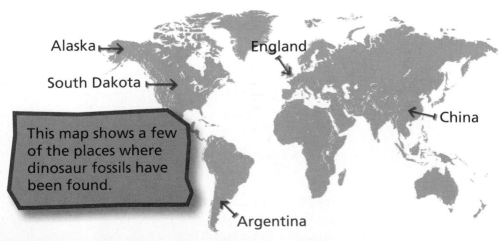

Alaska

South Dakota

England

China

Argentina

This map shows a few of the places where dinosaur fossils have been found.

From Fossils to Skeletons

While paleontologists are always interested in the latest fossils to have been excavated, many scientists study fossils in collections and museums, to see what new things they can learn. Sometimes they make discoveries about dinosaur species that were first identified more than a hundred years ago. And sometimes what they discover is a mistake!

Do you remember the fossilized *Iguanadon* tooth discovered by Dr. Mantell? When paleontologists first assembled an *Iguanodon* skeleton for museum display, they assumed that one of the dinosaur's fossilized bones was a horn that grew from its head, only to have later scientists make the discovery that the "horn" in question was a cone-shaped spike on the dinosaur's hand!

Such mistakes can involve more than one species of dinosaur, as sometimes the bones from different dinosaurs get mixed up. One time, scientists realized that the head of one kind of dinosaur had accidentally been put on the body of another dinosaur in a museum exhibit!

Paleontologists have to be very careful when assembling a dinosaur skeleton from fossils.

"Sue" is one of the most popular exhibits at the Field Museum in Chicago, Illinois.

Speaking of exhibits, you can learn a lot about dinosaurs by examining the dinosaur fossils that are on display in museums across the country. One of the most famous dinosaur exhibits in the world is found at the Field Museum in Chicago, Illinois, where the fossil skeleton of a *Tyrannosaurus rex* named "Sue" is on display.

Sue, named after her discoverer Sue Hendrickson, is the largest and most complete *Tyrannosaurus rex* skeleton yet found. Of the approximately 250 bones in a *Tyrannosaurus rex* skeleton, Sue is missing only one foot, one arm, and a few ribs and **vertebrae.** When Sue was discovered in South Dakota in 1990, it took six paleontologists two weeks to excavate her fossil from the ground, after which it took ten workers two years to clean the bones and piece the skeleton together!

What Sue Has Taught Us

Using computer technology, scientists have gained information from Sue that has caused them to change some ideas about *Tyrannosaurus rex*. For example, computer images taken of the inside of Sue's skull indicate that her brain was more than a foot in length, making it one of the largest of all dinosaur brains. The images also show that Sue had very large **olfactory bulbs,** which are sense organs used for smelling. Scientists used to think that *Tyrannosaurus rex* had a poor sense of smell, but the evidence furnished by the computer images indicates that the opposite was the case.

Most scientists believe that *Tyrannosaurus rex* was a fierce hunter, but the news about its sense of smell suggests that it might also have been a scavenger. Scavengers, which roam about looking for dead animals to feast on, are attracted to the scent of decaying animals. Was Sue a hunter or a scavenger? Scientists aren't sure yet. Sometimes new information presents more questions than answers!

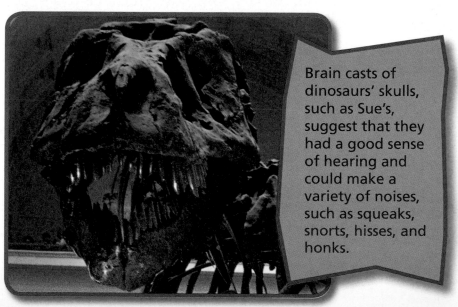

Brain casts of dinosaurs' skulls, such as Sue's, suggest that they had a good sense of hearing and could make a variety of noises, such as squeaks, snorts, hisses, and honks.

Birds of a Feather

The bird named *Archaeopteryx*, which is now extinct, was the size of a crow and flew short distances. Its fossils, which excavators have been finding embedded in layers of limestone in Germany since the nineteenth century, resemble those of dinosaurs. Some scientists think that *Archaeopteryx* served as a link between dinosaurs and birds. This link is important because it relates to a very interesting theory.

The theory is that, in a sense, some dinosaurs never became extinct! Of course, human beings will never get the chance to see an actual living dinosaur. But what the theory states is that modern birds are direct **descendants** of a group of meat-eating dinosaurs called **theropods.** Support for the theory includes the fact that theropods had eye openings and bone structures in their legs and feet that resemble those of modern birds. Like birds, theropods also laid eggs, and over millions of years their scales may have evolved into feathers.

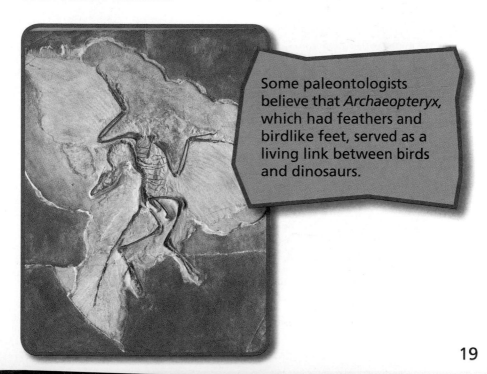

Some paleontologists believe that *Archaeopteryx,* which had feathers and birdlike feet, served as a living link between birds and dinosaurs.

What Caused the Extinction?

With each new fossil discovery, scientists learn more about dinosaurs. However, there is one mystery that may never be solved: Why did dinosaurs become extinct? The ancestors of animals as diverse as squid, turtles, and opossums all lived during the time of the dinosaurs. Why did they survive until modern times, while the dinosaurs became extinct?

For years, scientists have struggled to come up with an explanation for the dinosaurs' fate. Volcanic eruptions, diseases, and a gradual cooling of the Earth have all been cited as possible causes for the dinosaurs' extinction.

Opossum

Squid

Snapping Turtle

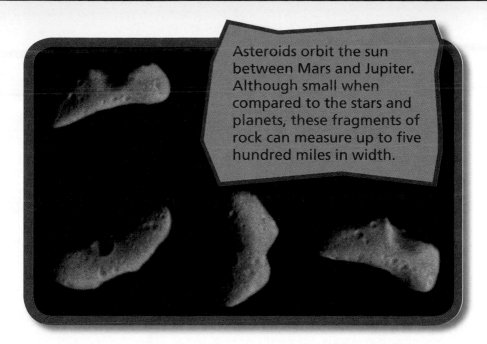

Asteroids orbit the sun between Mars and Jupiter. Although small when compared to the stars and planets, these fragments of rock can measure up to five hundred miles in width.

Many scientists now believe that the dinosaurs were made extinct by an asteroid that crashed into Earth millions of years ago. It is thought that this asteroid sent a huge cloud of dust and ash into the atmosphere, blocking sunlight for months or even years.

Scientists speculate that the cloud created by the asteroid's impact could have set into motion a catastrophic chain of events: First, plants would have died from lack of sunlight, then plant-eating dinosaurs would have starved, and finally the meat-eating dinosaurs would have died without any plant-eating dinosaurs to eat. Although a crater in the Gulf of Mexico and layers of Earth's rock strongly support this theory, scientists still have no direct evidence proving that an asteroid sent dinosaurs to extinction.

Dinosaurs lived on Earth for about 165 million years. In comparison, modern humans have lived on Earth for half a million years at best. Although dinosaurs will never again walk the Earth, the story of these amazing animals continues to fascinate all who read and learn about them!

Now Try This

New Dinosaur Fossil Discovered!

Imagine that you are a newspaper reporter who has been assigned to write an article about the discovery of a new dinosaur fossil. Follow the steps on the next page to create an image of the new fossil to go along with the article.

You can make a replica of an imaginary fossil and write a newspaper article about its discovery.

Dinosaur Discovery!

Last Wednesday afternoon, a paleontologist discovered a fossil believed to have belonged to a previously unknown dinosaur. The body fossil is a piece of preserved skin. The new dinosaur has been named . . .

1. Think about a body fossil or a trace fossil that would make an interesting discovery. Try to imagine one that would change popular theories about dinosaurs. For example, your fossil might change scientists' beliefs about a particular dinosaur's size, color, senses, or way of communicating.

2. Create an image of your fossil by making a pencil rubbing. To do this, take a piece of construction paper and draw the outline of a body fossil or a trace fossil on it. Then cut the shape out and cover it with a thin sheet of white paper. Rub a pencil over the shape and its edges. The outline will appear on the white paper.

3. Using either a computer or a separate piece of paper, write a newspaper article about the discovery. Include these facts:
   - where the fossil was found
   - a description of the fossil
   - a name for the dinosaur
   - what theories might change as a result of finding the fossil
   - quotes from scientists

4. Type your assignment so that it looks like a newspaper article.

5. Attach your pencil rubbing to the article and write a caption for it. Share your article with your class!

Glossary

avid *adj.* extremely enthusiastic.

carnivorous *adj.* living off of meat, being a meat eater.

collaborator *n.* person who works with another, usually in literary or scientific work.

consensus *n.* general agreement; opinion of all or most people consulted.

contention *n.* contest, competition.

descendants *n.* offspring; those born of a certain group.

herbivorous *adj.* living off of plants, being a plant eater.

olfactory bulbs *n.* organs located in the brain that are used for smelling.

theropods *n.* meat-eating dinosaurs that walked on two legs.

trackways *n.* a set of fossil footprints.

vertebrae *n.* the bones that make up a backbone.